math
exploration!

Using Math to Learn About the Continents

NUMBER CRUNCH YOUR WAY AROUND

AFRICA

Joanne Randolph

PowerKiDS
press™

New York

Published in 2016 by **The Rosen Publishing Group**
29 East 21st Street, New York, NY 10010

Produced for Rosen by Calcium

Editors for Calcium: Sarah Eason, Rosie Hankin, and Katie Dicker
Designer: Paul Myerscough

Art by Moloko88/Shutterstock

Photo credits: Cover: Dreamstime: Teckken Tan (top); Shutterstock: Erichon (back cover), Pius Lee
(bottom); Inside: Shutterstock: Bimbom 15tr, Bzzuspajk 11r, Pocholo Calapre 26r, Hector Conesa 20b, Sam
DCruz 17r, 19t, 19b, Chantal de Bruijne 6b, Pichugin Dmitry 7t, 9t, E2dan 16br, EastVillage Images 13br,
EcoPrint 4b, 9b, 29bl, Erichon 12br, 17t, Simon G 23c, Eric Gevaert 24b, 28r, Attila Jandi 21br, Oleksandr
Kalinichenko 7b, Iakov Kalinin 25r, Matej Kastelic 8c, Daleen Loest 27t, Xavier Marchant 23b, Martchan 5c,
15b, Mattiaath 13tl, Maggy Meyer 12bl, Andrew Molinaro 14t, Giulio Napolitano 21t, Noahsu 26l, Anna
Omelchenko 16t, 28t, Pecold 5t, Graeme Shannon 14b, Natalia Sidorova 23t, Mogens Trolle 18, Waj 11l,
Andrea Willmore 22bl, 29br, WitR 10t, Vladimir Wrangel 8t, Lara Zanarini 1, 27b, Oleg Znamenskiy 25bl.

Cataloging-in-Publication Data
Randolph, Joanne.
Number crunch your way around Africa / by Joanne Randolph.
p. cm. — (Math exploration: using math to learn about the continents)
Includes index.
ISBN 978-1-4994-1234-5 (pbk.)
ISBN 978-1-4994-1256-7 (6 pack)
ISBN 978-1-4994-1255-0 (library binding)
1. Africa — Juvenile literature. 2. Mathematics — Juvenile literature.
I. Randolph, Joanne. II. Title.
DT5.R36 2016
960—d23

Manufactured in the United States of America

CPSIA Compliance Information: Batch WS15PK: For Further Information contact Rosen Publishing, New York, New York at 1-800-237-9932

Contents

Africa   4

Second-Largest Continent   6

Deserts   8

Egypt and the Nile   10

Savannas   12

Mountains   14

Lakes   16

The Great Rift Valley   18

The Sahel   20

Coasts   22

Islands   24

An Amazing Continent   26

Math Challenge Answers   28

Glossary   30

Further Reading   31

Index   32

Africa

Africa is the second-largest **continent** on Earth. It has one of the world's largest deserts, the longest river, and the largest land **mammals**. It is known for its large **savannas**, too. We are about to begin an amazing math exploration of this continent using our best math and map skills. Are you ready?

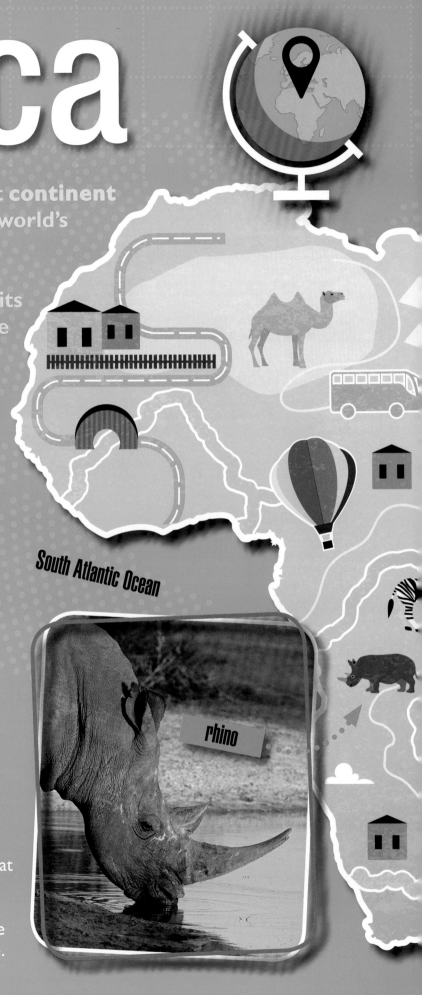

South Atlantic Ocean

rhino

How to Use This Book

Look for the "Map-a-Stat" and "Do the Math" features and complete the math challenges. Then look at the answers on pages 28 and 29 to see if your calculations are correct.

Africa's Regions

Africa's main regions include the Sahara, the Sahel, the Ethiopian Highlands, the savanna, the Swahili coast, the rain forest, the African Great Lakes, and Southern Africa. Each of these regions has different features and **habitats**. They also all have some unique plants and animals living there.

Kampala, Uganda

Map-a-Stat

Africa has the youngest population of any continent. Around 50 percent of Africans are age 25 or younger.

Africa has the second-largest population of any continent, with around 1.1 billion people.

Around 80 people per square mile (31 people per sq km) live in Africa.

Almost ⅔ of Africa's people live in **rural** areas.

Ethiopian women

Indian Ocean

DO THE MATH!

Use the information in red in the Map-a-Stat box to figure out the following challenge. How many of Africa's 1.1 billion people are aged 25 or younger? Here is the equation to help you solve the problem.

1,100,000,000 people x 0.50
(50 percent) = ? people

Complete the math challenge, then turn to pages 28—29 to see if your calculation is correct!

Second-Largest Continent

Africa is the second-largest continent after Asia. If you include its islands, it is 11.7 million square miles (30.3 million sq km). Algeria is the biggest country in Africa by area, but Nigeria has the biggest population.

Homo Sapiens

The earliest human, or *homo sapien*, skeleton was found in Africa. This human lived in Ethiopia around 200,000 years ago. Africa is believed to be the birthplace of the hominids, which are people-like **species** that include **modern** man.

Algeria

Ethiopia

Nigeria

Important remains of early humans have also been found at Olduvai Gorge in Tanzania, Africa.

Map-a-Stat

Africa is made up of 54 countries, plus 2 countries that are disputed, which means that not everyone agrees who should control them. It also has 10 **territories**.

It is believed that the first humans began leaving Africa around 130,000 years ago. These humans went on to populate the rest of the world.

Africa is joined to Asia in the northeast by a strip of land in Egypt called the Isthmus of Suez. The Suez Canal was created in the 1800s to improve trade between Asia and Europe. When it was first built, the canal was 101 miles (163 km) long. Today, it is 120 miles (193 km) long.

Suez Canal

Constantine is the third-largest city in Algeria.

DO THE MATH!

Use the information in red in the Map-a-Stat box to figure out the following challenge. How much longer is the Suez Canal today than it was when it was first built? Use this equation to help you.

120 miles − 101 miles
= ? miles longer

Complete the math challenge, then turn to pages 28–29 to see if your calculation is correct!

Deserts

Sahara Desert

Africa is the world's hottest continent and the third-driest. This means it has a lot of deserts. Deserts and **arid** land cover 60 percent of the continent. The desert areas include the Sahara Desert, the Kalahari Desert, and the Namib Desert.

The city of Ait Benhaddou is in north Africa.

Sahara Desert

The Sahara Desert is the largest hot desert in the world. Only Antarctica and the Arctic have bigger deserts. It is around 3.6 million square miles (9.3 million sq km) in area. It covers around one-fourth of the African continent. The northern part of the desert receives around 3 inches (8 cm) of rain each year. The southern part receives around 5 inches (13 cm). The Sahara Desert is a tough place to live, but many snakes, rodents, and scorpions survive there. The fennec fox, **jackals**, and **hyenas** live in the desert, too. There are also some cities there, such as Cairo in Egypt.

Sahara Desert

Kalahari Desert

Namib Desert

Map-a-Stat

The highest point in the Sahara Desert is the **volcano** Emi Koussi, which is 11,204 feet (3,415 m) high.

The Kalahari Desert is a sandy savanna. Its northeastern part is not classified as true desert. This is because it gets too much rain to be called a true desert. The driest parts get between 4-9 inches (10-23 cm) of rain, while the wetter parts can get up to 20 inches (51 cm) of rain.

The Namib Desert has been arid or semiarid for 55 million years, so many scientists consider it to be the oldest desert on Earth.

The Namib Desert has some tall sand dunes. Some are 1,000 feet (305 m) tall. The Sahara Desert has dunes that are around 600 feet (183 m) tall.

Fish River Canyon, Namib Desert

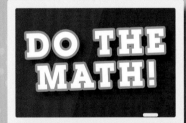
DO THE MATH!

Meerkats make their homes in the Kalahari Desert, digging tunnels beneath the sand.

Use the information in red in the Map-a-Stat box to figure out the following challenge. How much taller are the Namib Desert's tallest sand dunes than the Sahara Desert's tallest dunes? Use this equation to help you solve the math challenge.

1,000 feet – 600 feet = ? feet

Complete the math challenge, then turn to pages 28—29 to see if your calculation is correct!

Egypt and the Nile

pyramids at Giza

When people think of Africa, some of the first things that may come to mind are the Egyptian pyramids. The pyramids were built as tombs for **royalty** by the ancient Egyptian **civilization** between 2686–1650 BC. Ancient Egyptians lived along the banks of the Nile River, just as modern Egyptians do. Today, there are 86.9 million people living in Egypt. The two largest cities in the country are Cairo and Alexandria.

Alexandria

Cairo

Aswan Dam

Nile River

Lake Victoria

The Nile River

At around 4,132 miles (6,650 km) long, the Nile River is the longest river in the world. It flows through 10 countries. Surrounding the Nile are some areas of rich farmland. Much of the surrounding land is part of the Sahara Desert. A long time ago, the Nile River would **flood** regularly. This helped spread **fertile** deposits across the land surrounding the river, which helped plants grow. The Nile no longer floods land below the Aswan Dam, which was built in 1970. This has changed the land and it is not as farmable as it once was.

Map-a-Stat

More than 80 Pyramids have been found in Egypt.

The largest pyramid in Egypt is the Great Pyramid of Giza, also known as the Pyramid of Khufu. When first built, it stood 481 feet (147 m) high, but is now only 451 feet (137 m) high. Its base is 756 feet (230 m) long on each side.

A sphinx guards the Pyramid of Khufu. Khufu was a pharaoh, or king, of Egypt a long time ago.

Cairo is the capital of Egypt and the second-largest city in Africa.

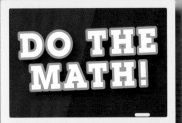

DO THE MATH!

Use the information in red in the Map-a-Stat box to figure out the following challenge. What is the perimeter of the base of the Great Pyramid of Giza? Use this equation to help you.

$$756 + 756 + 756 + 756 = ? \text{ feet in perimeter}$$

Complete the math challenge, then turn to pages 28—29 to see if your calculation is correct!

Savannas

Savannas are **grassland biomes**. In Africa, they cover a wide area that includes land from 28 countries. Like deserts, savannas in Africa tend to be dry, but they receive enough rainfall to support more plant and animal life than deserts.

lion

The Serengeti Plain

The Serengeti Plain has many different habitats, including savannas, woodlands, and open grasslands. Many animals you think of when you picture Africa live in the Serengeti. It has many mammal species, including zebras, wildebeests, elephants, giraffes, cheetahs, and lions. The plain is famous for the Great Migration of wildebeests and zebras. In spring, they **migrate** north to fertile **grazing** lands, then in fall, they head back to the southern grasslands.

Animals graze on the savanna in Kenya.

Map-a-Stat

Up to 400,000 zebras and 1.5 million wildebeests migrate from south to north and back again each year. It is a tough trip. Around 250,000 wildebeests die during the journey back south. They die from hunger, thirst, exhaustion, and from being hunted by lions, cheetahs, and crocodiles.

Savannas cover about 50 percent of Africa's land.

The savannas of Africa cover 5 million square miles (13 million sq km) of its total area, which is 11.7 million square miles (30.3 million sq km).

Giraffes make their homes on the Serengeti Plain and other African savannas.

the Great Migration

DO THE MATH!

Use the information in red in the Map-a-Stat box to figure out the following challenge. If 250,000 of the 1.5 million wildebeests die during the Great Migration, how many wildebeests survive? Here is the equation to help you solve the problem.

1,500,000 wildebeest – 250,000 wildebeest = ? wildebeest

Complete the math challenge, then turn to pages 28—29 to see if your calculation is correct!

Mountains

Most people picture deserts and grasslands when they think of Africa. However, Africa has many mountain ranges. Ethiopia has 50 percent of Africa's highest mountains. Tanzania is home to several ranges, including the Mahale Mountains and the Udzungwa Mountains. It is also home to Africa's tallest mountain, Mt. Kilimanjaro, which is 19,340 feet (5,895 m) high.

chimpanzee

The Ethiopian Highlands

There are two main ranges that make up the Ethiopian Highlands. These are the Simien and Bale ranges. The Great Rift Valley, which you will read more about later, lies between these ranges. Ethiopians grow coffee and a grain, called teff, on the slopes of the mountains. Many animals make their homes in these ranges, too. Some of them include the gelada **baboon**, the walia **ibex**, and the Ethiopian wolf.

Simien Mountains

Ethiopia

Mt. Kilimanjaro

Bale Mountains

Mt. Kilimanjaro is Africa's highest mountain.

Tanzania

Udzungwa Mountains

Mahale Mountains

Map-a-Stat

The Mahale Mountains are home to some of the last remaining wild chimpanzees. There is a population of 900 there.

The Ethiopian wolf is a symbol of Ethiopia. Sadly, it is almost **extinct** with only about 440 wolves remaining.

The Udzungwa Mountains are home to more than 400 species of birds. They also have a beautiful waterfall, called the Sanje, which falls 558 feet (170 m).

the Sanje

People live in traditional ways in the Ethiopian Highlands.

DO THE MATH!

Use the information in red in the Map-a-Stat box to figure out the following challenge. If there are 440 Ethiopian wolves and they travel in packs of 6, how many packs of wolves are there in the Highlands? You will need to round your answer. Here is the equation to help you solve the problem.

440 wolves ÷ 6 wolves per pack = ? packs

Complete the math challenge, then turn to pages 28—29 to see if your calculation is correct!

Lakes

Africa has major lakes, called the African Great Lakes. These lakes were created when Earth's shifting **plates** caused deep cracks to form in Africa's **crust**. Some of the lakes are Lake Albert, Lake Edward, Lake Kivu, Lake Malawi, Lake Tanganyika, Lake Turkana, and Lake Victoria. Many African plants and animals depend on these lakes to provide them with the water they need to live.

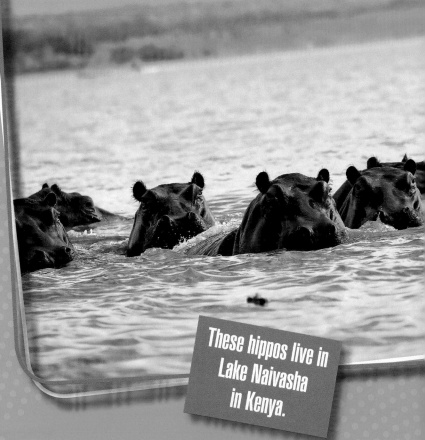

These hippos live in Lake Naivasha in Kenya.

Lake Victoria

Lake Victoria is Africa's largest lake and has an area of 26,828 square miles (69,484 sq km). By area, it is the second-largest freshwater lake in the world, after Lake Superior in the United States. Lake Victoria is one of the main sources of the Nile River. The countries Uganda, Kenya, and Tanzania border the lake.

Lake Albert
Lake Turkana
Lake Edward
Uganda
Kenya
Lake Victoria
Lake Kivu
Tanzania
Lake Tanganyika
Lake Malawi

Victoria Falls is 5,500 feet (1,700 m) wide.

Map-a-Stat

Lake Victoria has a shoreline of more than 2,000 miles (3,220 km).

Lake Tanganyika is the world's second-largest freshwater lake by volume, and the second-deepest after Lake Baikal in Siberia. Its maximum depth is 4,710 feet (1,436 m).

Lake Tanganyika's shoreline is 1,142 miles (1,838 km) long.

These fishermen are beginning their day at Lake Malawi.

Lake Nukuru

DO THE MATH!

Use the information in red in the Map-a-Stat box to figure out the following challenge. Though Lake Tanganyika is bigger by volume, how much longer is Lake Victoria's shoreline than Tanganyika's? Here is the equation to help you solve the problem.

$$2,000 \text{ miles} - 1,142 \text{ miles} = ? \text{ miles longer}$$

Complete the math challenge, then turn to pages 28—29 to see if your calculation is correct!

The Great Rift Valley

The East African Rift System runs from Jordan to Mozambique, covering a distance of 4,000 miles (6,400 km). A rift is a place where parts of Earth's crust are moving away from each other. Part of the East African Rift System is the Great Rift Valley in Africa.

Home, Burning Home?

The Great Rift Valley is a habitat for many plants and animals, including elephants and hippos. Most of these plants and animals live on the grasslands, by rivers, or on the slopes of mountains. There is one unlikely habitat in the valley, though. The valley has some lakes that are full of a **chemical** called sodium carbonate. This burns most living things. However, the lesser flamingo manages to wade in the waters without being harmed. It eats the tiny **algae** that live in the lakes. Thousands of flamingos feed in the Great Rift Valley's many lakes.

Flamingos feed at Lake Nakuru in Kenya.

Great Rift Valley

Indian Ocean

Map-a-Stat

If the 2 African plates that helped form the Great Rift Valley keep moving at their current rate, it will take 10 million years for a new **landmass** to break off.

The Great Rift Valley's highest point is 6,000 feet (1,830 m) above sea level. The lowest point in Africa is Lake Assal, which is 515 feet (157 m) below sea level.

Around 4 million flamingos make their home in the Great Rift Valley's lakes.

the Great Rift Valley in Kenya

Baboons make their home in the Great Rift Valley.

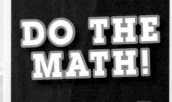

DO THE MATH!

Use the information in red in the Map-a-Stat box to figure out the following challenge. If you were to walk to the highest point of the Great Rift Valley at a rate of 4 feet per minute, how many minutes would it take you to reach the top? Here is the equation to help you solve the problem.

6,000 feet ÷ 4 feet per minute = ? minutes

Complete the math challenge, then turn to pages 28—29 to see if your calculation is correct!

The Sahel

Between the **Sahara Desert** and the savanna, there is a special habitat called the **Sahel**. It is semiarid and stretches from the Atlantic Ocean to Sudan. The Sahel area is found in a number of regions including parts of the Gambia, Senegal, Mauritania, Mali, Niger, Nigeria, Sudan, South Sudan, Burkina Faso, and Eritrea. It used to be home to many grazing herds of gazelle and **oryx**. Hunting and competition with livestock have pushed most of these animals toward extinction.

Red Sea

the Sahel

Atlantic Ocean

Women in Burkina Faso, in the Sahel region, head to work.

Climate

Like the rest of the Sahara Desert, the Sahel is very dry. It is said to have a semiarid **climate**, though, because it does have a rainy season. The southern part of the Sahel gets between 20–24 inches (50–60 cm) of rain each year. The middle area gets around 7 inches (18 cm) of rain per year. The northern part of the Sahel gets between 4–8 inches (10–20 cm) of rain each year.

Map-a-Stat

From the Atlantic Ocean to the Red Sea, the Sahel stretches 2,400 miles (3,862 km) across. The distance from the Atlantic Ocean to the Pacific Ocean in the United States is about 3,000 miles (4,828 km).

Between 1972 and 1984, 100,000 people in the Sahel died due to **drought**.

Tough plants, such as the acacia and baobab tree, grow in the Sahel. The baobab tree can have a trunk up to 30 feet (9 m) in diameter, and can be 159 feet (18 m) tall.

This is an arid area of the Sahel in Niger.

A woman carries her son to the market in Mali.

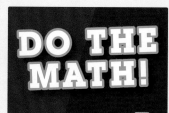

DO THE MATH!

Use the information in red in the Map-a-Stat box to figure out the following challenge. How much farther is it from coast to coast in the United States than it is in the Sahel? Here is the equation to help you solve the problem.

3,000 miles – 2,400 miles = ? miles longer

Complete the math challenge, then turn to pages 28—29 to see if your calculation is correct!

Coasts

Africa has a lot of coasts. Most of Africa's largest cities are in the coastal areas. Of the mainland countries with coasts, the mainland country with the largest stretch of coast is Somalia, with 1,880 miles (3,025 km) along the Indian Ocean. The country that has the least amount of shoreline is Democratic Republic of Congo, with only 23 miles (37 km) of coast.

Mediterranean Sea

Red Sea

Nigeria

Somalia

Atlantic Ocean

Democratic Republic of Congo

Indian Ocean

Cape Town is a large city in South Africa.

Nigeria

Nigeria is one of Africa's coastal countries. It is not the largest African country by area. However, it has the largest population and **economy**. More than 177 million people live in Nigeria. Its biggest industry is oil, but it also has thriving **telecommunications** and financial businesses.

Map-a-Stat

Though Africa is the second-largest continent and it has 16,000 miles (26,000 km) of coastline, it does not have a lot of inlets, or indents, in its coast. This means that it has less coastal area than the much smaller European continent.

Africa's coasts have a rich **resource** of fish and other ocean life. These fish provide food and employment for many Africans. In fact, around 10 million people in Africa work for **fisheries**.

Monastir, Tunisia, sits on the Mediterranean Sea.

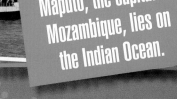

Maputo, the capital of Mozambique, lies on the Indian Ocean.

Lagos, Nigeria, is the largest city in Nigeria and an important port.

DO THE MATH!

Use the information in red in the Map-a-Stat box to figure out the following challenge. If you were in a boat sailing around Africa's coast at 10 miles per hour, how long would it take you to circle the coast? Here is the equation to help you solve the problem.

$$16{,}000 \text{ miles} \div 10 \text{ miles per hour} = ? \text{ hours}$$

Complete the math challenge, then turn to pages 28—29 to see if your calculation is correct!

Islands

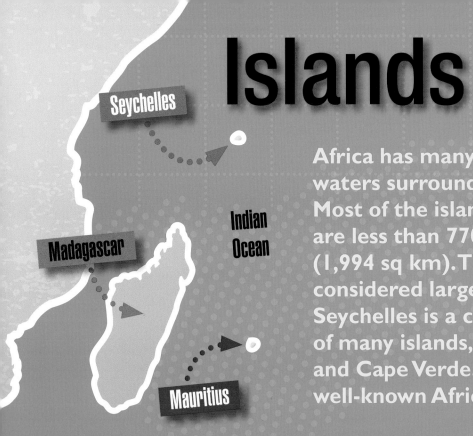

Seychelles

Madagascar

Indian Ocean

Mauritius

Africa has many islands in the waters surrounding the continent. Most of the islands are small, and are less than 770 square miles (1,994 sq km). The only island considered large is Madagascar. Seychelles is a country made up of many islands, as are Comoros and Cape Verde. Mauritius is a well-known African island.

Madagascar

Madagascar is Africa's largest island. It is also the fourth-largest island in the world. Many unique and interesting animals make their home on Madagascar. More than 23 million people do, too. The island has many different habitats, from deserts to fertile **plateaus** used for growing rice and other crops. It also has hot, steamy rain forests.

Lemurs are mainly found on Madagascar.

Map-a-Stat

Around 70 percent of Madagascar's wildlife is found nowhere else on Earth.

There are around 103 species of lemurs living on Madagascar.

Seychelles is made up of 115 islands.

Madagascar has around 258 bird species, and around 115 of them are found only on the island.

Most of Africa's islands are in the Indian Ocean, but there are a few in the Atlantic Ocean, too.

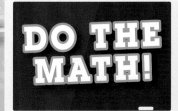
Many people visit Seychelles to enjoy its beautiful beaches.

Mauritius is a tropical island ringed by mountains.

DO THE MATH!

Use the information in red in the Map-a-Stat box to figure out the following challenge. If there are 115 species of birds in Madagascar that are found nowhere else on Earth, how many of its 258 bird species can be found in other places? Here is the equation to help you solve the problem.

258 species − 115 species
= ? bird species that also live on other continents

Complete the math challenge, then turn to pages 28—29 to see if your calculation is correct!

An Amazing Continent

Africa is an amazing continent. It covers around one-fifth of the planet's land area and has 15 percent of Earth's population. As the "cradle of humanity," it is the place where modern humans began. Africa also has some of the most fascinating animals in the world, with gorillas, hippos, lions, cheetahs, hyenas, lemurs, and many more.

gorilla

Vasco da Gama sailed around the Cape of Good Hope in South Africa.

Exploration

Africa gave birth to the first humans, and then some of those humans left to explore and settle new lands. That itch for discovery stayed with humans. In the 1400s, Europeans, who were looking for resources and **trade routes**, began to further explore the coasts of Africa. The voyage led by Vasco da Gama from 1498–1499 was the first to sail all the way around the southern tip of Africa to reach India. The trip made it easier to trade with Africa, Asian countries, and Pacific Islands, which had spices and other goods Europeans wanted. Today, Africa still has goods that are very valuable, especially oil.

Map-a-Stat

Vasco da Gama's first voyage from Portugal around the Cape of Good Hope to India and back took 2 years. In that time, he sailed 24,000 miles (38,600 km) and spent 300 days at sea.

Africa has one of the largest mineral industries in the world, with 57 percent of the world's cobalt, 39 percent of its manganese, and 46 percent of its natural diamonds, to name just a few.

African elephants are the largest land mammals. These huge animals stand 11 feet (3.4 m) tall at the shoulder and can be up to 24 feet (7.3 m) long.

Many rural parts of Africa rely on solar panels for energy.

elephant

DO THE MATH!

Use the information in red in the Map-a-Stat box to figure out the following challenge. If the distance around the **equator** is 24,901 miles, how many more miles would da Gama's crew have needed to sail to match this distance? Here is the equation to help you solve the problem.

$$24{,}901 \text{ miles} - 24{,}000 \text{ miles} = ? \text{ miles}$$

Complete the math challenge, then turn to pages 28—29 to see if your calculation is correct!

Math Challenge Answers

You have made it through the math exploration! How did your math skills measure up? Check your answers below.

Page 5

1,100,000,000 people x 0.50
= 550,000,000 people

Page 7

120 miles – 101 miles
= 19 miles longer

Page 9

1,000 feet – 600 feet
= 400 feet

Page 11

756 + 756 + 756 + 756
= 3,024 feet in perimeter

Page 13

1,500,000 wildebeest – 250,000 wildebeest
= 1,250,000 wildebeest

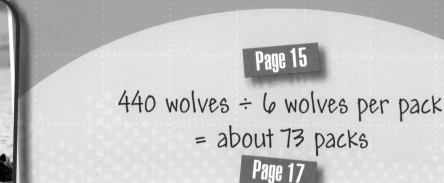

Page 15

440 wolves ÷ 6 wolves per pack
= about 73 packs

Page 17

2,000 miles – 1,142 miles = 858 miles longer

Page 19

6,000 feet ÷ 4 feet per minute = 1,500 minutes

Page 21

3,000 miles – 2,400 miles = 600 miles longer

Page 23

16,000 miles ÷ 10 miles per hour
= 1,600 hours

Page 25

258 species – 115 species
= 143 bird species that also
live on other continents

Page 27

24,901 miles – 24,000 miles
= 901 miles

DO THE MATH!

Glossary

algae Tiny plantlike organisms that live in water.

arid Very hot and dry.

baboon A type of large monkey with a snout like a dog's.

biomes Large areas of land with similar plants and animals.

chemical A substance that is used in or produced by a chemical process.

civilization A people who have an organized society.

climate The kind of weather a certain area has.

continent One of Earth's seven large landmasses.

crust The outer, or top, layer of a planet.

drought A long period of time in which an area receives little or no rain.

economy The system of how money is made and used within a particular region or country.

equator An imaginary line around the middle of Earth.

extinct No longer existing.

fertile Describes ground that is rich and able to produce crops and other plants.

fisheries Companies that make money from catching and selling fish.

flood When water spills out of a river and onto the surrounding land.

grassland A large area of land covered by grass.

grazing Eating grass.

habitats The surroundings where animals or plants naturally live.

hyenas Carnivores that live in Africa and Asia and eat the remains of dead animals.

ibex A type of wild goat found in the mountains of Europe, Asia, and Africa.

jackals A dog-like wild animal found in Africa, Europe, and Asia.

landmass A huge area of land.

mammals Animals that have warm blood and often fur. Most mammals give birth to live young and feed their babies with milk from their bodies.

migrate To move from one habitat or location to another.

modern In recent history, not ancient.

oryx A type of antelope.

plateaus Large, flat areas that are at higher altitude than the surrounding regions.

plates The moving pieces of Earth's crust, the top layer of Earth.

resource Something that people need to live, such as fuel or food.

royalty Kings, queens, princes, princesses, and anyone related to a royal family.

rural Areas that do not have towns or cities.

savannas Areas of grassland with few trees or bushes.

species A single kind of living thing. All people are one species.

telecommunications The science and technology of communication.

territories Particular areas of land that belong to and are controlled by a country.

trade routes Routes along which people bought and sold goods.

volcano An opening in Earth's crust through which ash, gases, and melted rock are forced out.

Further Reading

Books

Foster, Karen. *Atlas of Africa* (Picture Window Books World Atlases). Mankato, MN: Picture Window Books, 2008.

Friedman, Mel. *Africa* (True Books). Danbury, CT: Children's Press, 2009.

Hirsch, Rebecca. *Africa* (Rookie Read-About Geography). New York, NY: Scholastic, 2012.

Lonely Planet. *Africa: Everything You Ever Wanted to Know* (Not for Parents). Oakland, CA: Lonely Planet, 2013.

Schaefer, A. R. *Africa* (The Seven Continents). Mankato, MN: Capstone Press, 2006.

Websites

Due to the changing nature of Internet links, PowerKids Press has developed an online list of websites related to the subject of this book. This site is updated regularly. Please use this link to access the list: **www.powerkidslinks.com/me/africa**

Index

A
African Great Lakes, 4,
  16–17
Alexandria, 10
Algeria, 6–7
Antarctica, 8
Arctic, 8
Asia, 6–7, 26
Aswan Dam, 10

C
Cairo, 8, 10–11
coasts, 4, 20–23, 26
crops, 10, 14, 24

D
da Gama, Vasco, 26–27
deserts, 4, 8–10, 12, 14, 20,
  24
drought, 21

E
Egypt, 7–8, 10–11
Ethiopia, 4–6, 14–15
Ethiopian Highlands, 4, 14

F
flooding, 10

G
grasslands, 12, 14, 18
Great Migration, 12–13
Great Rift Valley, 14, 18–19

H
habitats, 4, 12, 18, 20, 24
humans, 6–7, 26

I
islands, 6, 24–26

K
Kalahari Desert, 8–9

L
lakes, 4, 10, 16–19

M
Madagascar, 24–25
Mahale Mountains, 14–15
mountains, 14–15, 18, 25
Mt. Kilimanjaro, 14

N
Namib Desert, 8–9
Nigeria, 6, 20, 22–23
Nile River, 10, 16

P
population, 5–6 15, 22, 26
pyramids, 10–11

R
rainfall, 8–9, 12, 20
rain forest, 4, 24

S
Sahara Desert, 4, 8–10, 20
Sahel, 4, 20–21
savanna, 4, 9, 12–13, 20
Serengeti Plain, 12–13
South Africa, 22, 26
Southern Africa, 4, 26
Suez Canal, 7
Swahili coast, 4

T
territories, 7
trade, 7, 26

U
Udzungwa Mountains,
  14–15
United States, 16, 21

V
volcano, 9

W
wildlife, 4, 8–9, 12–16,
  18–20, 23–27